I0472152

Leadership

The Comprehensive Guide to Become a Successful Leader in Every Area of Your Life

David Barron

Golden Road Publishing

Table of Contents

Introduction

Thank you for taking the time to read this book.

Leadership: The Comprehensive Guide to Become a Successful Leader in Every Area of Your Life covers the topic of leadership, and will teach you effective ways to achieve any leadership goal.

At the completion of this book, you will have a greater understanding of what leadership is really about (it's not what you think) and you'll learn the strategies you need to lead successfully and become a more competent leader!

Once again, thanks for downloading this book, and I hope you find it to be helpful!

David Barron

Chapter 1: A Leader with a Purpose

So many people dream of becoming leaders. Unfortunately, they have this misconception that leadership equates to power, fame, and fortune. Yes, you may see leaders that are powerful, famous, influential, and wealthy. However, leadership is not just all about these traits. There is actually so much more to it than meets the eye. When you become a leader, you become more than just a person who others look up to for their money, status, or influence.

When you hear the word 'leadership,' it already creates a significant impact on you. A word so simple is also so hard to execute. It is not easy to be a leader. It is not as glamorous as it seems. When you lead others, you have to know how to follow as well. You see, a good leader is also a good follower. Even more, you have to make certain sacrifices for the good of those you lead.

If you want to be a good leader, you need to have a purpose. This way, your leadership will be purposeful. People are not fond of so-called accidental leaders or leaders who do not possess the right characteristics. You have to aim to be like the leaders who are successful, yet remain unassuming and humble. These people are passionate about their visions, which are real and purposeful. They aim to reach such visions with a passion and their leadership is focused on achieving it.

The Meaning of Leadership

Leadership can be situational. Thus, you should never think of it as something that applies to everything. The truth is that there is no single way to lead people effectively in any given situation. Every person is different and has different needs. In the same way, every leader is different and has to adapt to the characteristics or personalities of the people that they lead.

A successful leader needs to have the right tools for the job. He/she also has to be prepared for ambiguity. After all, there is no book or manual that tells you how to be an efficient leader. You can never tell exactly how the people would think and behave. You just have to be ready for whatever comes along.

Leadership exudes a great aura. When you see a leader, you can immediately tell if he is good or bad. A good leader emits an aura that he knows what he is doing. You just get the feeling that this person is capable of leading. You do not even have to approach him just to know that he is a leader. He already exudes the vibe.

Leadership can be personal. There are people who have the ability to supervise others even when they are hundreds of miles away. In the same manner, they may be able to manage teams even from another office. If you want to be a good leader, you should be able to get along with the people you lead.

For starters, you should be able to make eye contact as well as develop a sense of trust among the members of your team. You can only achieve this when you form a personal connection with these people. It is not possible to order other people to speak or behave in a certain way unless you know them on a personal level and they feel that you have a personal relationship with them.

Then again, you need to exert time and effort to be able to form a personal relationship with anyone. You cannot claim that you know someone when you have just met that person. You also cannot form a relationship if your efforts and intentions are half-hearted. You have to actually care about the person in order for you to be able to form a genuine relationship with them. Moreover, you need to have their best interest in mind.

There are leaders who are genuinely passionate and enthusiastic about what they do. Because of this, others connect their vision with them and automatically respect them as their leaders. You should strive to be a leader like this; someone who does not have to force others to follow, respect, or give you attention.

The Personal Nature of Leadership

As you have read, it is not easy to be a leader. You can only be a good leader when you stop your incessant attempts at automating performance reviews. Do not even try to make things easier than they are. Instead, you have to go for something that is more relevant. Keep in mind that a bad performance management process will not get better with automation.

Performance reviews are also evidentiary. Therefore, there is no way for you to convince other people that automating efforts could yield in better worker performance. You have to stop trying to automate things and embrace simplification. You have to make things more relevant to employees and managers so that you can eventually drive worker performance and bring more success to the company.

Leaders cannot be virtually developed. A lot of people have this misconception that that is possible. Today, everyone has access to a computer, smartphone, or any other electronic device. The Internet is available in various places all over the world. Very rarely that you will see a person who does not know what the Internet is, or has never used it before.

Due to the advanced technology that we have today, most human interactions are done online. This includes seminars, lectures, and business meetings. People prefer to connect with others virtually instead of meet with them face-to-face. This is not surprising since this tends to be the more convenient way. No matter where you are in the world, you can communicate with other people via the Internet.

Then again, you still cannot be a leader if you watch video seminars or webinars online and yet you do not understand what they are truly about. The Internet is an excellent medium for reinforcing skills, but it has no power to reinforce skills that are not inherent in a person. In other words, you cannot learn new skills by simply relying on the Internet. You can use the video seminars to guide you and further enhance the knowledge and skills that you already have, but they cannot help you develop such skills.

Since leadership is personal, its development is also personal. So, if you really want to be a leader, you have to attend workshops, facilitated sessions, and face-to-face coaching. It is not enough to just read books or watch instructional videos on leadership. You need to have an experience of leading people for you to be able to claim yourself as a leader.

You have to realize early on that there is no shortcut to leadership. You can use online tools for your convenience, but they are only supplementary. Also, your leadership should have a purpose in order for it to take off. You need to have a demonstrated vision as well.

Everything Changes When You Live and Lead with a Purpose

There are days when you think about your purpose in life. You wonder if you even have a purpose or if you were just put into this world for no reason at all. During these days, you become bothered and uneasy. You become restless because you do not know what you have to do next. Many people are also having the same dilemma, and just like you, they are wondering what they are doing here on Earth.

Victor Strecher, a behavioral scientist at the University Of Michigan's School Of Public Health, suffered an unfortunate loss. In 2010, his young daughter, who had a rare heart condition, suddenly had a heart attack and died. She was only nine years old.

After this, Strecher has been filled with thoughts regarding the purpose of his life. He started to wonder what his life is truly about. He also started questioning how life should be lived. Because of the many thoughts he had on his mind, he decided to write a book entitled *Life on Purpose*.

The book is both meditative and inspirational. It talks about the nature of purpose. It tells you how philosophers from different generations have debated the connection between happiness and purpose. Do you become happier when you know what your purpose in life is? The book also contains inspirational stories of real people who were able to find their purpose in life, as well as personal confessions from the author himself.

According to Strecher, it is possible for you to measure the strength of your life's purpose. You can also measure how strong your goals and values are. Likewise, you can measure your plans to make a difference in this world. All of this correlates with your psychological wellbeing. You can even consider these factors as markers of longevity and health.

Researchers say that for every one-point increase on a six-point scale measuring the purpose of life, people with heart disease reduce their likelihood of a heart attack by 27%. This is good for two years. Older people, on the other hand, can reduce their likelihood of a stroke by 22%.

Even though it is not totally clear how the purpose of your life can impact such results, it is still feasible that they can be connected to stress. Many studies have shown that stress is associated with numerous health conditions. It can also effect people at a cellular level.

There is a study in which the researchers studied the way meditation affects the genetic health of mothers who experience high levels of stress. The researchers measured their telomeres before and after they went to a mindfulness meditation retreat. The stress levels of these women are so high, but not all of them attended the said retreat.

Those who showed up were divided into groups – one that served as the control group and the other that practiced mindfulness meditation. After the mindfulness meditation retreat, the researchers discovered that those who went were able to make their telomeres longer. This means that their health significantly improved after taking part in the retreat.

Most people will think that the mindfulness meditation made them this way. After all, mindfulness meditation has many great benefits. However, the researchers have discovered that it was not really the increased mindfulness that made the telomeres of the women longer, but rather their improved sense of purpose in life. The mindfulness meditation only served as a means for them to achieve such a sense of purpose.

You, too, can be like these women. You can also improve your health by finding out what your purpose in life is. You can also practice mindfulness meditation in order for you to achieve clarity of mind and be able to discover your purpose in life.

Strecher added that schools and workplaces should teach the positive effects of achieving a sense of purpose so people would be encouraged to find their own purpose in life. When you are aware of why you are alive and where you are, you would be able to act accordingly. You will know what you need to do to improve the quality of your life further, as well as inspire other people.

If you teach students how to find their purpose in life, you will help motivate them to do their best in school. They will continue to strive to get better grades even though they are not particularly excelling in certain subjects. They would use the adversities and challenges that they go through as lessons, which can be beneficial to their lives.

Likewise, if you teach employees how to find their purpose in life, you will help them become more proactive as well as encourage them to work for a good cause. They would also view their workplace as a place with tons of great opportunities instead of a place where they suffer and get exhausted. Take note that most employees also prefer companies that value a sense of purpose.

People preferring to work in a place where having a sense of purpose is valued is not really surprising. According to one study, those who are employed in hospitals are 45% more likely to wash their hands and practice good hygiene while on duty if they know that doing that will help patients prevent diseases. This is because they are genuinely willing to help save other people's lives.

Putting Your Purpose Into Action

You should take note that merely discussing your purpose in life with other people is not enough. Your words are senseless if you do not put them into action. This is why you need to practice what you preach. Your purpose in life should reflect your values and goals. Also, you have to remember that there is a difference between knowing what your purpose in life is and actually taking action to fulfill it.

According to Strecher, the process of aligning such purpose with yourself is a dynamic process. It requires both your willpower and energy. It is not enough to use just one. You can compare this to being in a boat. If you wish to move forward, you need to have wind that can blow the sails. However, you also need to have a strong rudder that can prevent the wind from blowing your boat off-course.

The same is true with your life. You can only move forward if you have both willpower and energy. Do not worry about not having them. You already have them. You just need to harness them so that they can serve their purpose. For example, you can modify the way you lead people. You can also change the way you make decisions in the office.

Of course, you should not neglect your health. If you are in top shape, you can come up with better decisions and take better care of your employees. You can take care of yourself by having the right diet, exercising more often, and getting a sufficient amount of sleep each day. You should also focus more on the present through mindfulness meditation, yoga, and other similar activities.

Remember that your willpower, purpose, choices, and energy are all bidirectional. Each one of them has an influence to one another. So, it only makes sense to know what your true purpose in life is. This way, you can engage in more productive activities that can help you figure out what your purpose in life is.

Purpose can actually be more elusive than you think. The culmination of individual experiences and personal interactions in your lifetime can be considered as a purpose. Nevertheless, you may still have a hard time fostering purpose.

In spite of this, you should continue to examine your life more deeply. You should exert an effort to strengthen your desire to be of help and service to other people. You should aim to contribute positivity into the world. It is better to try to do something than not do anything at all. If you do not do anything, you can suffer from even worse consequences.

Become a Person of Influence and Attempt to Make a Difference

You can be a leader or a follower, but you can also be both. A leader is someone who leads and acts as a role model to other people. A follower is someone who obeys the leader and follows orders. What differentiates a good leader from a mediocre leader? What separates the best leaders from the rest?

You do not need to be the smartest, richest, or most powerful person in order to be an effective leader. You have to start from within. You have to start by finding your purpose in life. Only then will you be able to know what you have to do in order to be an effective leader.

According to Richard Leider, a vitality expert and coach, purpose refers to the deepest dimension within yourself that tells you who you really are, where you are heading to, where you are from, and why you even exist. If you do not show that you are passionate about the things that you care about, people will not think that you are genuine about your leadership, and they will not want to follow you.

Your purpose makes you a leader that is capable of inspiring people and changing lives. A purpose-driven leader always wants to connect with something that is much larger than life. Microsoft's founder, Bill Gates, did not aim to make billions when he first started his company. All he wanted was to use computers to help transform the lives of people.

He knew his purpose in life and he pursued his passion. While doing so, he became one of the richest and most influential person on the planet. He did not mean to be the richest. It just occurred as a result of him going after what he is passionate about – helping people change their lives for the better.

Apple's founder, Steve Jobs, is also known all over the world. Without him, you will not even be using your iPhone right now. Apple's computers are sought after everywhere. Many people do not mind lining up for hours just to get their hands on the latest Apple products. They are even willing to stay overnight outside of stores.

Just like Bill Gates, Steve Jobs had no intention of creating personal riches for himself, but rather it happened as a byproduct of him producing value for others. He wanted to encourage people to show their creative side so that they may enrich their own lives. He aimed to use his products as tools to help these people. He also knew what his purpose in life was and he also decided to go after his passion. Because of this, he was able to successfully connect people with one another and dramatically change the course of human history.

Chapter 2: Effective Leadership

In this day and age, it is more common to see pay cuts, budget cuts, furloughs, and layoffs than job vacancies and hiring opportunities. The morale of employees is usually low. Even though they were not included in the long list of laid off workers, they are still not thrilled to be at work. Because of this, their productivity is affected in a negative manner. Their satisfaction with the company and their position also decreases.

In fact, many employees tend to lose hope and faith in capitalism as a whole. It is during these times that a lot of managers and executives look for a place to hide for safety. They hide because they do not want to face their employees as well as their profit losses. This is not a good way to lead people. If you want to be a good leader, you should not imitate these behaviors. If you lead your employees effectively, their commitment and satisfaction will increase. This will cause them to increase their productivity, even during tough times.

Zenger Folkman took the liberty to collect data from 100,000 direct reports from different organizations. This data was used to determine the effects of leaders on the job satisfaction and commitment of their employees. Every direct report contains a rating of the effectiveness of the immediate manager as well as the level of satisfaction or commitment of the employee.

In the study, forty-nine behavioral items assessed the effectiveness of the leaders. They also evaluated sixteen competencies in leadership. The employee satisfaction or commitment index is the one that measured the extent to which the employees experienced satisfaction with their organization. It also measured the level of confidence they had within their organization, as well as their level of commitment and likelihood to stay.

Once the combined dataset of leadership behaviors and levels of employee satisfaction and commitment were collected, the researchers isolated the leadership behaviors that proved to be the most influential when it comes to making committed employees satisfied. By determining the critical dimensions, you can focus better on actions that can have a huge impact on your business.

Leadership and Emotional Intelligence

In 2014, author Simon Sinek wrote a book entitled *Leaders Eat Last*. It was inspired by the time he was studying the Marine Corps and finding out why they are willing to trust their lives with one another. For Sinek, the closeness of the marines can teach leaders and help them become more efficient at what they do.

When he went to the Marine Corps' mess hall, he noticed that the most junior eat first while the leaders eat last. Although there is no written or spoken rule about this order, the leaders consciously eat last because they believe that it is their responsibility to put the needs of other people above their own.

In the workplace, employees become happier and more engaged when they are treated with respect. As a leader, you can show that you respect your employees by listening to them and understanding their situation. You should show that you do not merely care for them on a professional level, but on a personal level as well. The best leaders develop a personal relationship with their followers.

In a study done at the Center for Creative Leadership, results showed that work performance and empathy are interrelated. The latter has a positive impact on the former. Researchers have discovered that the managers who are more empathic towards their employees are able to perform better at work. If you do not think that you are empathic enough, do not despair because empathy can be learned. Also, the more you practice empathy, the better you get at it.

Leadership Styles

Leadership comes in different styles. The style you use in your workplace determines the way your employees perceive you. It is important for you to be mindful of your perception since it is often reality.

Authoritarian

With an authoritarian type of leadership, decisions are exclusively made by top management. Those who are below them do not have any right to question their decisions. While this type of leadership is pretty common in different businesses, it also generally creates a culture of fear. It causes employees to feel scared to voice out their opinions, provide feedback, or give suggestions.

Transactional

With a transactional type of leadership, also referred to as the carrot and stick approach, the leader considers the actions of his employees as transactions. So, if an employee does his work properly, he gets rewarded. It is a highly transactional kind of leadership style, without much emotion involved.

Democratic

With a democratic type of leadership, the leader allows the employees to take part in the decision making process. He also tries to make the workplace as equal as possible. Due to the inclusiveness of this type of leadership, the employees are generally happier and more productive. However, there may be situations in which the employees take advantage of their leader for his kind nature. This is why it is important to ensure that only the right people are hired.

Laissez–Faire

With a laissez–faire type of leadership, everyone is more relaxed. The leader gives full control to the employees when it comes to what decision they want to have and to what kind of work they want to do. However, this type of leadership needs to involve a lot of trust. The leader has to trust that his employees would do the right thing.

Leadership Mistakes

In order for a business to prosper, the right kinds of leaders should be hired. The following are the leadership mistakes that have to be avoided:

1. A tough or sudden transition.

A person should not get a promotion without adequate training or receive one too quickly. The transition from employee to manager can be difficult. In fact, it is usually among the biggest challenges that new managers have to face. If ever you are promoted too soon and you are experiencing some difficulty, you should take time to adjust to your new role. Do not hesitate to open yourself up and learn from other people, even if those people directly report to you. You should also read as much as you can so that you can improve your knowledge. Simply being mindful that this is such a huge transition is a vital step to successfully overcoming it.

2. Lacking a consistent approach to performance management.

Performance reviews typically have a negative reputation because managers tend to focus their attention on those who perform poorly as a result of a lack of time. This should not be the case. Managers should give their attention to all the employees as well as help each and every one of them to improve their career. In case this happens to you, you can fix it by attending meetings frequently. You have to make sure that you have meetings on a regular basis, especially one-on-one meetings every month. This will ensure that you give every person adequate attention. Yes, it may take a lot of time, but it is necessary in the development of employees.

3. Not enough communication.

Employees generally look to their managers for support and guidance. If there is a lack of communication, confusion may arise. Employees would also waste valuable time. You have to realize that too much communication does not exist. You need to take time to prepare emails, presentations, and summaries. You need to have adequate communication within the company in order for things to work smoothly. If communication lines are open and transparent within an organization, more ideas can naturally develop and there will be less animosity amongst co-workers.

Key Things to Focus On

As a leader, you may experience some difficulty in finding out where you need to focus your attention on. You will face a lot of challenges throughout your term. However, you should especially focus on certain things, such as the following:

1. Gather feedback from the members of your team.

You need to constantly communicate with your team members, including and telling them to provide you with feedback. This way, you would know what you can do to make things better and what the company can do to improve the things around the workplace. You have to look for a way to both gather feedback and take immediate action. You can use a variety of employee feedback tools to help you make the process much easier and more convenient.

The fact that you ask your employees for feedback is already an indication that you value their opinions and care about them. At times, simply doing this is already enough to improve their satisfaction at work. Keep in mind that the most important part is to eliminate any fear that your employees may have. You also have to encourage them to honestly and openly speak their mind.

2. Have one-on-one meetings on a regular basis.

When you speak with your employees face-to-face, you show them that you are willing to communicate with them on a more personal level. This is much better than merely sending out an email or talking to them through conference calls and video seminars. A one-on-one meeting allows you to form a bond as well as strengthen the relationship that you have with the members of your team.

There is no better communication strategy than a one-on-one meeting with your employees. It allows you to connect better with each one of them to ensure that they are happy and satisfied in the workplace. It also allows you to learn about any issues that might be going on and help them deal with such issues before they go out of control.

Inform them that the meeting is not a progress report or update. It is simply an informal discussion to ensure that they are satisfied with their work in the company.

3. Set clear goals.

One of the most vital aspects of employee satisfaction is setting clear goals that everybody can resonate with. If there is lack of clarity in terms of goals or job descriptions, employees will most likely be unhappy. They might even be tempted to quit their jobs.

The Objectives and Key Results (OKR) is a highly popular framework for goal setting. It is measureable and simple. Through this system, you can set a high level and vague objective such as 'becoming the thought leader in employee engagement.' You can use two to three key results to reach that objective, such as 'publish five blog posts' or 'speak at four conferences.' These basic examples show how measurable these goals are and how easy it is for you to tell if you can reach them or not.

4. Acquire new knowledge often.

As a leader, you have to learn many things on a consistent basis. You have to regularly read books, magazines, or articles, as well as immerse yourself into new things to gain more experiences. When you know a lot of things, you can help your team grow. You can also be an inspiration to your employees.

As much as possible, you have to learn more about emotional intelligence, dealing with employees along with their issues, technical information, and many other things. This way, you can provide an answer every time a member of your team asks a question.

If you want to be a leader who is well rounded, you have to make time for reading and learning. You have to mark your calendar and set a schedule for reading a particular book or doing a specific activity that can help you improve your knowledge and experience.

5. Seek a mentor.

You may already know a lot since you are a leader. However, you should realize that you are not perfect and that you do not know everything. With this being said, you should consider getting a mentor. You need to look for a person who can help unleash your untapped knowledge and potential. Your company would surely benefit from this once it's unleashed and utilized.

This is why it is ideal for companies to come up with mentorship programs in order to help workers reach their maximum potential. These mentorship programs should pair up new employees and senior employees. Lower-performing managers can also be paired with top-performing managers. With help from a mentor, you can be a better leader.

Leadership Development Programs

All the major talent management functions have a part in comprehensive leadership development programs. They can be supported by unified talent management technology platforms. Such functions include recruitment, assessment, performance management, career planning, and development.

Recruitment is helpful in sourcing leadership talents. Assessment is helpful in evaluating internal and external leadership capabilities. Performance management can help monitor and create course corrections, which are necessary for the development of leaders. Career planning is meant to help employees understand and know more about their leadership options so that they can set development goals. Succession planning is meant to avoid any leadership gaps in the future. Finally, there is development, which is necessary for creating a roadmap to fill in skill gaps.

Successful leadership development programs generally start with the alignment of leadership developing the overall strategy of the company as well as an understanding of the kind of leadership style that is necessary for executing such a strategy.

So, in summation, a leadership development program involves the following steps:

1. Determining the most suitable style of leadership for the organization;

2. Identifying the potential and current leaders in the company;

3. Identifying the gaps in leadership; developing succession plans for roles that are critical;

4. Developing career planning goals for leaders with potential;

5. Developing skills roadmaps for leaders in the future;

6. And developing retention programs for both future and current leaders.

Chapter 3: Character

In order for you to become a better leader at work, you need to have character. According to Bernard Montgomery, a British Field Marshal, leadership is the will and capacity to rally women and men to a common purpose as well as the character that results in confidence.

How much do you know about character? For starters, actions are its real indicators. Words are nothing without actions. If you say one thing and do another, you only show that you are not a credible leader.

For example, in the office, suppose for a moment that you told your staff to arrive at 7:30 a.m. for an urgent meeting. You told them that it is very urgent and that you would be there at 7:00 a.m. to wait for them. They showed up on time but you were an hour late. What does this say about your character and credibility?

Also, if you promise your employees a raise and do not follow through, how do you think they will think and feel towards you? Even in seemingly simple things such as having a Christmas party in the office and then cancelling at the last minute does not make you a leader with character.

If you keep doing this, your employees will no longer believe you. They will think that you will just let them down again. Not only that, but you will also discourage them and make them lose their morale. They will no longer be satisfied working in the company.

When they have problems or issues, they might hesitate to come to you for guidance or advice because they do not trust you anymore. They also do not trust your leadership skills and personality either. Instead of getting closer to you, they will start to drift away.

Also, you should know that talent may be a gift. Character, however, is a choice. It brings lasting success. A person who wants to be successful needs to have strength of character. You may be a highly talented person, but if your character is weak, you will not succeed in your career.

For example, if your business goes down and you need to let some employees go, do you have the courage to break the sad news in their face or do you hide somewhere else and let things move through their course? If you have a strong character, you would face the reality and do your best to fix the situation. If you already did your best and you still have to let your employees go, you should tell them what happened and break the news to them face-to-face.

You have to let your employees know the truth about the company. You should not leave them when the boat is sinking. It is even worse if they just found out that the company is doomed when everything is already falling apart. As a leader, it is your responsibility to always be there for your employees.

You can also become a better leader by inspiring and motivating everyone in the workplace. As you may have noticed, leaders who are effective at motivating and inspiring other people have a high level of enthusiasm and energy. They empower the members of their team to overcome difficult circumstances and improve the level of their performance.

Many leaders concentrate on fulfilling the tasks indicated in their job description. Because of this, they often forget to be an inspiration to their employees. You should not be like these leaders. Keep in mind that if there is no inspiration in the workplace, your employees will not be motivated to do their job well. They may procrastinate or just lose their focus and energy. All of these factors can take a toll on their level of productivity.

Then again, if you focus on inspiration too, you will be able to unlock another level of energy and effort, which can make a huge difference in the line between failure and success. Your company will be able to improve its ratings or sales. In other words, you need to find a way on how to inspire your employees so that they can perform at their best.

Chapter 4: Charisma

Some leaders are introverts while others are extroverts. As a leader, being an extrovert can pay off really well. However, this does not mean that you cannot get along well with people if you are an introvert. You just have to be charismatic. Do not worry because this trait can be learned. With charisma, you can be more persuasive, inspiring, and influential. Other people will be magnetically drawn to you. They will trust you and will want to learn from you.

Robert House, an emeritus professor of organization studies at The Wharton School at the University of Pennsylvania, said that charismatic leaders somehow inspire their followers to be highly committed to their mission. They become willing to make sacrifices as well as perform above and beyond their call of duty.

To become a charismatic leader yourself, you need to form a connection. You should not just lead by authority. You also have to level yourself with the members of your team and connect with them from different angles. This could be easier if you share a particular interest or view with them. There is no need for you to make them feel like you are the boss or that you are in control of everything. If you are genuinely charismatic, people will connect with you instantly.

Rather than focus on yourself and your demands alone, you should occasionally ask your employees if they are satisfied with your leadership skills. You should ask them if they believe that you are going in the right direction. Encourage them to ask questions, such as what their comfort level at accomplishing a certain task is. Listen to their responses and learn from them. You should only do this occasionally though; there is no need to do it every time.

Another way to be charismatic is by keeping things light yet productive. Can you ease everybody in the room? Can you keep tension at bay by using light humor yet still remain productive? Charismatic leaders know how to achieve balance. They are not too serious. They also know how to be in a light mood by using humor. Nonetheless, they know about boundaries. After laughing, they get back to work.

A charismatic leader is also confident. This is why people believe what a leader says without a doubt. They speaks with confidence and captures the attention of everyone in the room. They have a commanding voice that makes everybody listen. They also manage to convince others to believe what he says even if they have previously believed otherwise.

In spite of their greatness, a charismatic leader is humble. A charismatic leader is alright with not being the smartest person in the room. They do not get insecure if they do not know something that another person knows. They brings confidence to the members of his team by encouraging them to speak their minds.

For example, during meetings, do you do all the talking or do you allow other people to step in and state their suggestions and opinions? Do you take criticisms positively or negatively? Are you open to feedback? If all you do is take over everything, then you are not a good leader. You also have to listen to what your employees have to say. Listen to their suggestions and thank them for giving their input. If the idea is good, then you should consider taking action to execute it. If the idea does not sound plausible, you should still thank the person for giving input and do not humiliate them in front of everyone else.

Furthermore, a charismatic leader is strongly committed to his/her goals. He inspires to lead through example and is well aware that his own commitment to his goals is vital to team motivation. He is prepared to take on all levels through hard work and passion.

Chapter 5: Commitment

Commitment is what separates the doers from the dreamers. It refers to the dedication to a certain organization, belief, cause, or willingness for involvement. A leader who is committed to his company always shows up, follows through, and sticks with it. If there are more people committed to the organization, there is a greater momentum generated to get things done.

Commitment is actually the backbone of an organization or group. It is what gives your organization strength. The more committed you and your employees become, the more effective all of you become at influencing other people. When all of the people in your company act with commitment and determination, more people will give you their attention.

As a leader, you can show your commitment by not being discouraged easily. You must not give up, no matter how difficult the situation becomes. You also have to set an example to those who do not have the experience or confidence to go through difficult times. Take note that people tend to cooperate at higher levels when they share their commitment. It is commitment that fosters trust, care, and camaraderie, which are all necessary to keep an organization going.

Say, for example, one of your employees comes up to you and informs you that he is going to be late in submitting a project. If you are truly committed to this employee, especially since he has already done a lot for the company in the past years, you may feel disappointed. However, you will also take into consideration certain factors such as he may have other things to do or perhaps the project is too much to deal with. Instead of getting angry, you may offer this employee some help.

Then again, if you are only half-heartedly committed to this person, you will point fingers and blame him. You will also begin to think of the past mistakes or poor work that he has done in the past. You will forget all the hard work this employee has put into the company. As a result, you will feel negatively towards this person. You may even feel that this kind of situation is already "expected" of that employee.

If you are committed to your employees, you are loyal to them and you trust them. You do not mind going out of your way just to see the good in them as well as provide them with your own energy and time so that they may succeed. If your employees are also committed to you, they will do the same. They stay loyal to you and they become willing to make sacrifices to help you.

When the level of commitment goes down, people turn cynical. They begin to search for faults and flaws. They also stop exerting effort to help one another. You have to realize that as a leader, a commitment model is necessary for your leadership. You need to gain commitment from the members of your team.

Likewise, the members of your team should be committed to you in order to trust your decisions. They should also be willing to give you their energy and time to help you achieve the goals of the team. Team members who do not have faith in their leader tend to question every little request as well as hold back. When your team has strong levels of commitment, you are able to go above and beyond. This yields great results for your team.

Chapter 6: Communication

Without ample communication, your organization will not succeed. Developing good communication skills is necessary for effective leadership. As a leader, you have to be able to share ideas and knowledge, as well as send a sense of enthusiasm and urgency to other people. If you are not able to clearly get your message across to motivate other people to act on it, then your message will be pointless.

How often do you communicate with the members of your team? It is crucial for you to communicate with them often. You have to provide them with real-time feedback, have one-on-one monthly meetings, and ensure that you are open to questions and suggestions at all times.

Improving Your Communication Skills

In order for you to have effective communication skills, you need to have trust. It is important for you to build trust with the members of your team. You have to be honest, straightforward, and open to them. In addition, you have to be mindful of your words or tone and body language.

Words or Tone

You should be mindful of the words and tone that you use in your speech because they can have a significant effect on the way the members of your team receive your message.

For example, imagine that one of your employees enters the room and you said in an upbeat tone "thank you for joining us." Then, another employee walked into the room twenty minutes late, so you said in a regular tone, "thank you for joining us."

Essentially, the words you said are the same. However, they conveyed two different meanings because of the tone of your voice.

Body Language

During Amy Cuddy's TED talk titled *Your Body Language Shapes Who You Are*, she discussed the way body language affects the way people perceive you. According to her, your body language has a significant effect on the way you make judgments.

These judgments can predict significant outcomes such as who you promote or hire.

In a study done by Nalini Ambaday, a researcher at Tufts University, it was found that when people view the thirty-second soundless clips of physician and patient interactions, they judged the physician according to how nice he is and not to how competent he is. So, if the physician is nice, they think that he will not be sued. They did not factor in his level of competence. All they put into consideration was whether or not they like the person and the way the person interacts with others.

Giving Feedback

It is important for you to give feedback to your employees, whether via informal chats or formal performance reviews. This way, they will know how they are doing and they can improve certain areas of their work. It lets you help them grow professionally. Also, giving your employees feedback will let them know that you care about their work.

When you give feedback, however, see to it that you make and maintain eye contact. You have to lean in slightly. If you lean away, you signal hostility. Refrain from crossing your arms. You have to bring your hands towards your chest as well as touch your fingers together. You may also put your hands on your lap.

Do not make it personal. As you know, human psychology is greatly involved in the giving of feedback to employees. Keep in mind that your employees can be highly sensitive. Thus, it is important for you to show compassion when you give feedback. Whenever you give feedback, always make sure that you do not give a personal attack. You need to focus on the behavior and not the person.

For example, when you are giving feedback to an employee, you can tell him that his presentation would probably have had more impact if only he had used a bolder font. You should not tell the employee that his work is not good because this implies a personal attack.

You also have to be specific. In order for your feedback to have a significant effect, you need to make it as specific as possible. Refrain from being vague since this will only make the behavior less likely to change. You may also want to give specific recommendations for improvement.

Refrain from using the "feedback sandwich." It refers to the idea of sandwiching negative feedback between two positive ones to make the negative feedback seem less hurtful. You may think that this seems like a good idea: you get to convey your message and the employee does not get hurt. Well, you are wrong. This kind of strategy will not work because if the negative feedback is so vague and deeply buried in the positive feedback, so much so that the employee may not notice it and not get the message. Thus, you need to be straightforward and honest with your employees.

Furthermore, you have to have a change of mindset. It is crucial for you to approach feedback with a mindset that is rational and logical. You have to be coaching and helping instead of scolding. When you change your mindset, you will be able to approach delivery. Your follow-up and feedback will also be better.

When talking to your employees, you have to find out how you can help them improve. Here are some questions you can ask:

1. How can I improve as a leader?

2. What is your most challenging task?

3. What can be done to help you succeed?

4. Do you want to work on certain projects when given a chance?

5. Is there anything that prevents you from getting work done?

6. What can be changed during team meetings that can make them more effective?

7. Do you need more coaching or help in a certain aspect of your job?

8. Do you feel happy that you are here?

9. How can you rate your work and life balance at the moment?

10. What can be done to increase your happiness level?

11. What can be done to improve your relationship with your co-workers?

12. What do you think is the best thing about working here?

Chapter 7: Competence

According to John Maxwell, competence is much more than words. It is the ability of the leader to say, plan, and take action in a way that other people know that he knows how.

Leadership competencies refer to leadership behaviors and skills that contribute to leadership performance. Through competency-based approaches to leadership, companies can form and create their new set of leaders much more effectively. Researchers have defined the essential global competencies and leadership competencies, but future business strategies and trends should still drive the formation of new leadership competencies.

It is true that certain leadership competencies are crucial to every firm. However, organizations should also define the leadership attributes that are distinctive to specific organizations in order to form (or maintain) a competitive advantage.

The Essential Leadership Competencies

When you focus on skill development and leadership competencies, you can promote a more effective leadership style. Then again, you should take note that the skills necessary for a certain position can still change depending on the level of leadership within the organization.

Your organization can find out the levels and positions that require specific competencies through a competency-based approach. According to researchers at the Center for Creative Leadership, they divided the overall structure of the essential leadership competencies.

When it comes to developing and choosing leaders, HR professionals have to consider the competency level of the individual as well as compare her to the people who need to further develop theirs. When you look at the current competency level of this person and verify if his skills are suitable for a leadership position, you are able to make better decisions for hiring, promoting, and developing leaders.

You can tell that a person has a capacity to lead an organization when she is able to manage change, solve problems and make decisions, manage politics and influence other people, take risks and innovate, set visions and strategies, manage work, enhance business knowledge and skills, and understand and navigate an organization.

You can tell that a person is capable of leading himself when he shows integrity and ethics, displays purpose and drive, exhibits leadership status, increases his learning potential, increases his self-awareness, develops adaptability, and manages himself.

You can tell that a person can lead other people when he can communicate effectively, develop others, values difference and diversity, builds and maintains relationships, and manages effective work groups and teams.

The Global Leadership Competencies

The development of effective global leaders is one of the competitive advantages for multinational organizations. Aside from essential global competencies, the global leaders experience challenges that need more competencies. In other words, a global leader has to be a person who is able to cultivate business in foreign markets, set business strategies at a global level, and manage globally-diverse teams.

The Conference Board research report stated that 73% of managers say that global leadership and domestic business leadership are different when it comes to their required skills. The challenges that these leaders face include the management of different employee groups as well as business processes. They also have to approach challenges and problems in an adaptive manner. In addition, they have to adjust to new cultures and values, as well as adapt to various kinds of personal and business stressors.

In order to address the challenges faced by global leaders, experts and researchers determined the global leadership competencies can contribute to their success. These global competencies include being able to develop a global mindset, having respect toward cultural diversity, and having cross-cultural communication skills.

A person can be said to have global executive competencies when she is flexible and open minded in both tactics and thought; displays cultural sensitivity and interest; is able to handle complexity; is resourceful, resilient, energetic, and optimistic; has integrity and a stable personal life; is honest; and has value-added business or technical skills.

Chapter 8: Passion

Passion refers to an intense range of emotions, such as joy, anger, and hatred. Ironically, it is usually connected to what happens to leaders when they do not have it. In leadership, it gets linked to creativity loss, lack of energy, burnout, or reduced motivation.

As a leader, why do you need passion? First of all, passion allows you to focus your energy on causes that align with your core values. Your natural gifts and talents, and personality are tapped into your passion. Also, you have to help other people learn about their passion so that you can put the members of your team in situations that can help them motivate others.

Passion is like an interest on steroids. People who have self-awareness consciously strive to live their passions as well as channel their desires. Passion is like a tightly-woven thread of inner concern that forms a rope strong enough to help you reach your dreams.

Sadly, there are quite a lot of leaders who do not have enough self-awareness in terms of understanding their passion. Always keep in mind that you have to know and understand what your passion is if you want to be a good and effective leader.

The Connection Between Passion and Vision

Vision is known to be crucial in leadership. Some people say that it is a common denominator in leaders. Others claim that it is the driving force in their desire to be influential to other people. Well, if vision refers to what you see as a leader, it is passion that enables you to see what is important. If vision is not linked to passion, it is mechanical. If it is linked to passion, it becomes inspirational.

For example, if you are trying to promote a vision for a cause that you are not truly passionate about, it will resonate in your actions and words. People will be able to tell that your heart is not fully dedicated to whatever cause you are trying to promote. At work, you can convince your employees to donate books to public libraries. However, if you are not fond of reading yourself, your attempts may seem hollow. Even though you are trying to contribute to a good cause, you will not be able to convince people because you are not truly passionate about it. The words and tone that you use, your body language, and actions will tell the whole truthful story.

Many leaders understand intuitively that effective communication requires vision and passion. If passion is not sufficient, however, you may think that you can use intensity as a substitute. This is not a good move. Your employees will know and see the difference. When you use intensity alone, you will seem to say that you want the members of your team to believe what you are saying. On the other hand, if you use passion, you tell your employees that you really believe what you are saying.

Simply put, intensity is generally marked by emotion while passion is marked by conviction. Also, intensity comes with hype while passion is packaged with authenticity. At the same time, intensity seems superficial while passion seems natural. Furthermore, intensity is communicated by loud talking while passion is communicated by plain talking. Although you can be intense with your leadership, you should never use intensity to substitute for passion.

A Passionate Leader

Passions come from the issues and interests that you want to learn more about, take part in, pay a price for, or recruit other people to pursue.

As a leader, you have to know the difference between issue-based passion and interest-based passion. Some people go with interest-based passion because they find it fun and pleasurable. There are people who love leisure activities such as golf, tennis, and painting.

Other people go for issue-based passion because they feel that it gives them a sense of fulfilment and purpose. These people are usually the ones who care for the environment, the homeless, and leadership. They tend to promote causes that let them leave a legacy behind.

Every person has issue-based and interest-based passion. A leader who does not have any room for pleasure tends to put his legacy at risk in the long run. Oftentimes, interest-based passion is linked to activities. Thus, it flows from a mixture of an acquired skill or natural ability and an interest. People generally like things that they are good at. Likewise, they tend to be good at things that they like.

An issue-based passion is generally linked to causes. Thus, it tends to come from experiences. Those who are passionate about the homeless and poor, for instance, can point to formative experiences where these people's needs have been imprinted on their hearts.

As a leader, you also have to realize the difference between strategy and passion, especially since it is related to issue-based passions. You see, variety is beautiful. People can have a similar passion and yet have different approaches to fulfilling it. Keep in mind that your passion may require more than a single approach. Hence, you have to be careful not to turn your allies into your enemies by not valuing their strategies when you have a similar passion.

In addition, you need to search for ways on how you can mix issue-based passion and interest-based passion in order to come up with incarnation passion. For instance, a person who is interested in music may sing and play the guitar. If he also has an issue-based passion for social justice, he may combine both passions and form a band such as U2. Incarnational passion is lived in real-life roles or situations. On the other hand, if his issue-based passion is connected to his faith, he may want to be a worship leader.

So, this only proves that passion is necessary for leadership. You need to find which areas you are passionate about so that you can concentrate on them. Authors Louis Patler and Robert Kriegel did a study that involved 1,500 participants. The study lasted for over twenty years. It was about finding your passion in life and seeing its value.

In the beginning of the study, the participants were divided into two groups. Group A consisted of 83% of the participants. These people chose a career that allowed them to make enough money so that they can do whatever they want later on in life. Group B consisted of 17% of the participants. These people chose a career that allowed them to go after their passions and not worry about money until later on in life.

After twenty years, the results were shocking and thought-provoking. The researchers found that 101 out of the 1,500 total participants became millionaires, with 100 of them coming from Group B. These people were the ones who decided to pursue their passion and not worry about money.

Based on this study, you can tell that a passionate leader is energetic, drives vision, ignites other people, and raises influence. A passionate leader is driven forward. He has enough energy that allows him to lead himself and other people. Energy is not existent without passion and nothing exists if there is no energy. So, a passionate leader brings energy to everything he does.

If you want to see your goals and visions being fulfilled, you need to have passion that drives your vision's results and production. The vision of your team or organization must passionately and frequently be communicated to other people. Even if you do not say it, people will know that you are a passionate leader when you are able to ignite others. Just as John Wesley had said, if you set yourself on fire, other people will love to see you burn.

So, if you are a passionate leader, you will be able to gain more influence. Other people will desire to be a part of your team because they want to know what is going on. You need to be passionate in order for you to be more influential. Furthermore, you gain more potential when you are passionate. Having passion lets you open doors towards success as well as gain more opportunities. This happens because you are able to move closer towards your potential when you are passionate about what you do in your personal and/or professional life.

Chapter 9: Problem Solving

According to John Maxwell, a leader can be measured by the problems that she faces and deals with. She searches for problems that are her size. So, if you choose to deal with small problems, then you are not capable of solving big problems. On the other hand, if you are not afraid to tackle major issues, then you are a leader who does not give up easily and is able to handle the pressures that come with tackling huge problems.

If you want to be a leader with good problem solving skills, you can start by reading more books. According to a study published in the peer-reviewed journal *Science*, reading books, particularly literature, can improve your theory of mind. It is a skill that refers to your ability to find out what other people think, believe, want, or intend.

You should also watch other people. You can actually do this during your free time, such as when you are waiting in a long line or stuck in traffic. Just look around and watch the people around you. Think of what they can possibly be going through. If you do this often, you will be able to improve your level of empathy.

See to it that you also work on non-verbal cues. For instance, if a person talks to you, you should try to see how you react. Do you just sit there without feeling any emotions? Do you move your eyes around a lot? Do you fidget in your seat? Or do you do something else? A good leader listens intently to the speaker. You cannot say that you are a good leader if you do not listen and pay attention.

How to Be Good at Problem Solving

A good leader is a good problem solver. He takes proactive measures in order to avoid conflict. He also addresses issues whenever they arise. The best leaders in business use problem solving tactics that allow them to deter problems and peacefully resolve them when necessary.

First of all, you need to be transparent in your communication with the members of your team. If there is a problem, you need to be able to make everyone comfortable in expressing their opinions and concerns. Effective leaders are able to facilitate open forums as well as work for the accountability of the whole team.

Problems in the workplace tend to come from company boundaries. If you can break these boundaries, you will be able to decrease competition and create an open culture. As a leader, you need to understand and act on this in order to lessen the problems that you have in the workplace.

You have to foster a culture that is open-minded too. In essence, problem solving is all about everyone coming together to work as one for the organization. You can achieve this by having open-minded employees.

See to it that you have plans of action all the time. A successful leader is an experienced problem solver. Every time there is trouble, he already knows what to do. He has had a lot of experiences in the past that he already knows what options he has. Keep in mind that the worst way you can approach the problem is not having any underlying strategy. You need to take your time, step back, and evaluate your situation.

With all the problems around, you may think that you do not have sufficient time to solve them without facing adversities on your way. These problems can grow bigger and bigger, and you may find yourself taking a shortcut in order to alleviate tension points temporarily. If this is the case, you cannot move on to another problem and find a solution for it. You have to solve the cores of these problems so that you can prevent being caught up in a never ending cycle that prevents you from finding feasible solutions.

As a leader, problem solving is the essence of your existence. Your main objective is to reduce these problems. You need to have the courage to deal with them before things get out of hand. You have to be resilient in your mission to create and maintain the momentum for your company and employees. At work, you may find it quite difficult to deal with workers who make things more complicated due to their envy, ploys, power plays, self-promotion, and corporate politicking. Other factors that may affect productivity include lack of resources and budget, silos, and a variety of other circumstances.

Oftentimes, your competitors may give you problems when they convert long-standing clients, form new industry relationships, and launch new products, strategies, or brands. Acquisitions and mergers keep you on your toes as well as further distract you from being able to solve your problems by making new ones.

Karl Popper, a very influential philosopher of the twentieth century, once said that life is all about problem solving. The best leaders in the world are actually those who are best at problem solving. They are patient and they step back so that they can view the problem from a wider perspective and with a circular vision. They view around, beyond, and beneath the problem. They look at what is beyond what is obvious. They use lenses of opportunities to approach their problems.

On the other hand, those who do not have enough wisdom tend to approach their problems with a linear vision. They only see the problem when it directly lies in front of them. They are not able to see the possibilities that can be found in the problem. Because of this, they are not able to realize the totality of what their problems represent. They do not realize that every problem is essentially the same and just packaged differently.

As a leader, you should not see your problems as distractions, but rather as strategic enablers for more opportunities and improvements that you have not yet had before.

For example, if you are planning to launch a food business, you should be prepared for problems. You may experience issues with labels, packaging, and shipping. This can affect a certain percentage of your initial shipment. Since you have just launched your business, your clients may still be testing your products. If they liked it, they would continue to do business with you. Otherwise, they would stop.

When you experience issues, it is natural to be in a panic mode. However, instead of panicking, you should take on the necessary problem solving approach. You need to find out what steps you need to take so that you can effectively deal with your label supplier, trucking company, manufacturer, and client.

You should not view your problems as hurdles that can make you lose clients and sales. Instead, you should take proactive measures to show people that you are capable of finding a solution and taking action. In addition, you would prove that you can respond efficiently and promptly with comprehensive step-by-step incident reports that include your changed management efforts.

Chapter 10: Relationships

In the most basic sense, if you get along with people, they will get along with you as well. Seems pretty simple, right? Knowing how to mingle is actually the most crucial ingredient in success. This is according to former United States president Theodore Roosevelt. Every person has something in common with another person, and that is the feeling of being special. People like it when they are complimented. It makes them feel better.

As a leader, you have to know how to make your employees feel better so that they can be more motivated to work for you. A leader who keeps in touch with the concerns and issues of the members of his team tend to yield higher levels of commitment and satisfaction amongst employees. This kind of leader is seen as someone who is able to get results while also showing concern for the needs of other people. He is able to create a strong positive relationship with the members of his team.

Quality of Relationship

It is not enough to form a relationship alone. You need to make sure that this relationship is of good quality. More importantly, you have to ensure that the quality of your interactions is strong and positive. Do your employees feel better after talking to you? Do you know how your interactions with employees affect them? You need to have high quality and frequent interactions with the members of your team so that you can have a strong relationship. You have to be mindful of the way you behave around your employees. Your emotional intelligence also matters.

Keep in mind that leaders who are relationship-driven tend to focus on people instead of power. According to statistics, women outnumber men at work. In the past, there were more men, particularly white men, in the workplace. Today, however, this hierarchical model has changed. Women have been recognized and their skills were found to be increasingly valuable to the company, which is a positive trend.

Nevertheless, as organizations continue to face rapid change and globalization, their need for a more flexible and nimble model has increased. If you will look at the traditional leadership model, you will notice that teams tend to function based on the top-down pecking order. At present, this power-driven model is starting to weaken and more women are starting to excel and dominate the workplace.

Why does this happen? There is a huge possibility that it occurs because women are less driven by career and finances. They value personal fulfillment more so than their male counterparts. This is why they tend to create friendlier environments at work. This new workplace order is not merely about women and men though. It is about forming relationships. A leader who is relationship-driven can empower other people and realize that empathy is necessary to create a productive and strong team. This kind of leader also makes decisions using relationship-focused lenses instead of title-based perspectives.

The times are changing. The baby boomers are retiring and the millennials are entering the workforce. Thus, leaders should be able to adapt to such a changing world. Otherwise, they can risk losing employees who are talented and efficient. The younger employees tend to prefer leaders who are relationship-driven and possess a sense of community. They prefer leaders who they know will respect their opinions and ideas, as well as include them in the decision making process.

Relationship-Driven Leaders vs. Title-Driven Leaders

In the past, companies and organizations preferred to hire people who could make decisions in an objective manner. They considered these people to have a strong potential for leadership. Title-driven leaders usually take analytical approaches to problem solving when it comes to coming up with rational and fair solutions. Such kinds of leaders are usually well-versed at arriving at logical decisions. He works hard to analyze and implement results. Then again, he may also appear to be highly critical. He may also not realize it when his decisions or questions are beginning to alienate the other workers in the company.

On the other hand, a leader who is relationship-driven is more patient, tolerant, and empathetic. This kind of leader approaches the decision making process in a subjective manner. They make use of their personal values as guidelines as well as examine how every opinion can have an impact on other people. This kind of leader tends to be approachable and harmonious. They like to include every employee and build trust amongst them. In addition, this kind of leader is not afraid to admit when they are in the wrong. They take constructive criticism well. Also, they are also adept at forming personal connections. However, this kind of leader may sometimes seem too concerned with regard to what other people think of him. Some people may even think that he is too weak and not capable of making tough choices.

How to Adopt the Relationship-Driven Approach

Due to the changing times, leaders should adapt with change. As you may have already experienced, new generations of people are slowly taking over the workforce. With all the baby boomers out, the leaders in the industry should know how to deal with this new generation. Since they prefer a leader who is relationship-driven, you have to be a leader that is relationship-driven.

Even though you cannot change your innate personality, you can change your behavior. For starters, you can be more open towards varying points of views. A good leader makes sure that every member of his team is able to voice out their concern, suggestion, or opinion. You can solicit the perspectives of your employees with regard to how you can address new opportunities and challenges. You have to be open-minded when considering new and creative ideas, but you should not forget to consider traditional options too. You have to view the big picture before you dismiss an idea. When you have already evaluated all your options and came up with a decision, you can share your criteria with the members of your team so that they will see that you value their presence.

You have to know how to balance strong decision making with empathy. When you open yourself to new ideas, you should not make all your decisions based on consensus. You can say that you are a well-rounded and relationship-driven leader if you are able to use your skills to manage groups and individuals effectively. At times, consensus-building generates the most favorable outcomes. In some cases, you may have to deal with tough decisions and issues that do not please everybody else. You know that finding the right balance can be difficult. With coaching, however, you can learn the skill and be more comfortable with finding input while coming up with unpopular decisions.

You need to collaborate on issue management. If a project does not work out as expected, what do you think your reaction is? Do you tend to tell the members of your team that they did something wrong? Do you tell them how they can correct this mistake and prevent it from happening again? Do you allow the members of your team to lead during the debriefing process? Yes, it can take more time. However, a relationship-driven leader is able to ask the members of his team about their opinions with regard to the situation. He is also able to find out how they can take and execute upon a different approach next time.

The two different approaches can both have positive outcomes. However, the latter can better validate the viewpoint of the employee and deepen his/her relationship with you. During times of company stress, you may want to use a relationship-driven approach to minimize any negative reactions. In this case, you have to ask the members of your team to change their ways instead of ordering them to do so.

You also have to do better when it comes to employee development. Focusing on employee development also identifies employees who have a potential to improve as well as focuses on grooming the best workers. A leader who is relationship-driven strives to develop every employee, learn about their aspirations, provide them with feedback, and help them reach their goals.

As a leader, you have to meet with the members of your team on a regular basis so that you can discuss the strategies that work and the strategies that do not. You should also use these meetings to evaluate new training opportunities and challenges. When you aim to develop your employees, you get to improve your interpersonal skills too.

You have to realize that silence does not always equate to agreement. A person who stays silent is not necessarily agreeing. If nobody questions your decision, you should not think that every person in your team is supportive of it. Not everyone may agree with what you want. Sometimes, silence could mean resistance. Thus, you need to ask the members of your team and find out if they think that your decision can yield a positive result. If they do not think that it is such a good idea, you can use their feedback for guidance and adjustment. It can helpful in your decision making in the future.

Respect and empathy are actually just like the oil in a machine's wheels. A machine that is properly oiled tends to work better. Likewise, a successful leader knows that the company can perform better if there is employee empowerment and development. When you adopt a relationship-driven approach, you can earn the confidence and trust of your workforce.

Chapter 11: Responsibility

As a leader, you have to be responsible. If you cannot do that, you cannot lead your team. You have to keep in mind that leadership is about being responsible and not just being in power.

Robert Joss, the dean of Stanford University's Graduate School of Business, said that in every leadership role, there comes an informal dependence on others that is in a lot of ways more powerful and more important than the authority or power that the organizational chart implies.

Sadly, there are a lot of leaders who think that being a leader entitles them to power. They fail to realize that being a leader actually requires them to show responsibility towards the members of their team. There is no need for you to tell people that you are powerful. If you are a powerful leader, they will surely notice.

As a leader, you need to get the most out of each and every one of your subordinates. Plus, you need to get the members of your team focused. It does not matter if the goals are clear or not. You need to show them that you can lead the way. Do not allow them to see that you do not have any clue on what you need to do.

In addition, you have to remember that every team needs to have a strategy and a framework. You can take the steps necessary to improve your planning, organizing, and staffing. These steps will help you lead your team towards the right path. They bring focus and discipline to your company, and this is highly valuable. However, they do not have much to do with how your team feels and thinks, even though it has so much to do with how it acts. With this being said, you have to pull your team along through proper communication.

You have to explain your vision in detail. Refrain from being too general. You need to provide the specifics so that you can give the members of your team a sense of direction.

Of course, you need to gain the trust of your employees. You need to enlist your followers when you are on top. You are actually highly dependent on the people below you. You need members who are committed, inspired, and motivated. As their leader, you have to help boost their level of confidence.

Then again, there are also problems present when you are on top. When you are there, your employees may not tell you what you have to hear at all times. Now, this can be very difficult. Thus, you need to ask the right questions. Asking these questions is more ideal than merely dictating policies.

Moreover, you need to be open for any potential criticisms. You can organize town hall meetings or confidential surveys. You can also speak with the members of your team in private. Even if you are the CEO, you should still encourage employees to talk to you directly. When someone complains of a particular issue and that issue has been raised at least three times, then it is probably worth checking out. You need to figure it out and take action.

You also have to set your tone. For instance, pretend that a very unfortunate event happens and one of your employees is killed while on duty. Do you attend the funeral yourself or simply send representatives? Some CEOs will think that it may be intruding to go to the funeral.

However, you may actually be surprised that your presence can bring some sort of comfort to the family. They will appreciate it if the leader comes and pays respects himself. With this being said, being a leader is not really about you, but rather about your team. It is about your relationship with the members of your team.

Being Responsible: The Highest Mark of Leaders

Two individuals may have the same skills, educational attainment, and experience, but only one of them may be promoted. Why does this happen? Well, the willingness of a person to act responsibly is a major reason why this happens.

In a study conducted by Dale Miller, two sets of executives were studied. One of the groups was identified by colleagues as efficient and ideal for promotion. The other group, however, was initially perceived to be ready but was later found out to be unfit for the position.

Both groups were given a deck of sixty-two statements that described management behavior. They were told to sort this deck in a bell-shaped curve. It was arranged starting from the most effective to the least effective. The group that was found to be effective chose the statement "accepts full responsibility for the performance of the work unit." In fact, it was chosen so many times that it outdid statements regarding planning, delegation, time management, technical skills, and staffing.

Such selection also showed the distinction of the groups. The group that was thought to be initially ready but then discovered to be unfit did not have a strong attachment to responsibility or responsible behavior.

Responsible Behavior

You have to know that being accountable and being responsible are two different things. When you are accountable, you are willing to receive the results or outcomes of an activity or project. When you are responsible, you are willing to go much further. Do you make things happen because you are required by your job or you actually believe that you have to?

A leader who is responsible shows this behavior in different directions. It may affect how he behaves towards the members of his team. However, he is also just as strong as his immediate boss. As a leader, you need to have a good attitude and set of values.

For instance, when dealing with your subordinates, you have to show that you are willing to be in charge and stick with your decisions. You are not a member of the group. You are the leader. So, you need to accept the responsibility that comes with the role. With this being said, you need to change your daily routine. You should not resist the responsibility that defines your new role.

You should also stay on top of the problems. Refrain from assuming that someone else is going to step in and fix them for you. Being a leader also means that you need to have a results-based view. It does not really matter how good of a person you are. The level of your effectiveness is defined by the outcomes that your team yields. You are a responsible leader when you can make sure that your team can produce positive results.

When it comes to dealing with upper management, you have to accept criticism well. Instead of feeling negative about it, you need to take the necessary steps to improve. You have to find out how you can fix the problems as well as make amends with the people whom you have inconvenienced. You also have to serve as a buffer from the pressures that come from them, as well as fend off any unreasonable demands from other people.

When you deal with other departments, you have to make sure that you exhibit a responsible attitude. As a leader, you need to have an attitude of responsibility, which you can express in a variety of ways. This kind of behavior is nuanced and subtle, as well as palpable and important. You should feel proud when your company achieves success. Your personal goals should come second to the goals of your team.

Chapter 12: Security

Keep in mind that competence can never compensate for insecurity. If you are an insecure leader, you will not be able to succeed.

When Leaders Feel Insecure

A lot of people dream of becoming leaders. However, not everyone is fit to be one. Some people think that they are actually leading, but they are not. The nature of insecurity is deceptive because it hides many layers of propped up and built up self-esteem behind. It works behind the scenes to bring you down and render you irrelevant. You know that it is right there in your private and unguarded moments.

You may be an insecure leader when you think and feel that you are inadequate. It is true that no person is perfect, but you should not have a sense of deficiency or ineptitude that strips away your strengths. You are a secure leader even when you do not think that you are invincible. You are a secure leader when you are confident that you can do it. You do not go deep into self-doubt or lose your self-assurance.

You may be an insecure leader when you think and feel that you are incompetent. When you feel this way, you believe that you are not good enough to lead the members of your team and fulfill the duties of a leader. You do not think that you have sufficient knowledge and skills. You are a secure leader when you know that you are competent because you have what it takes to be a leader.

You may be an insecure leader when you think and feel that you are inconclusive. As a leader, you have to ensure that you truly know the vision that you want your members to grasp; you need to have good communication skills. Then again, this does not mean that you should never try to analyze situations. Once you have taken a particular course of action, you can move on with confidence that you made the right decision.

You may be an insecure leader when you think and feel that you are incomplete. There is this notion that there is a person who is a 'total package.' However, there is no such thing because nobody is perfect. Everyone has inadequacies and weaknesses, which can be filled by other people. When you surround yourself with people who are just as capable of leading as you are, you should not feel threatened. An insecure leader is threatened by people who are just as good or seem better.

You are a secure leader if you are not threatened by their personalities and skills. You should actually be thankful that there are other people who are well-trained and have a high capacity for performance. These people can help you out and you can learn from them. Likewise, they can motivate and inspire you. You have to be secure in your own skin. You have to feel secure enough to want other people to also succeed.

You may be an insecure leader when you think and feel that you are inconsequential. You have to realize that you are significant. You are an important person with talents. You have a mission to fulfill. Therefore, you should not let your insecurity take these good things away from you. You are a leader, so you matter.

You may also be an insecure leader when you think and feel that you are inferior. You should refrain from comparing yourself with other people. You have to stop wasting your time trying to figure out how to stack up against other people, especially other leaders. You have your own strengths. So, you should focus on your own leadership abilities. You have to be strong enough for your team.

Then again, you should not think and feel that you are superior either. Yes, you are the leader of the team and your members have to obey you. However, this does not make you a better person than them. As their leader, you have to be their mentor. You have to be a good example for them to follow. You should not act superior towards them, but rather act as a servant-leader who has their best interests in mind.

You may be an insecure leader when you think and feel that you are inhibited. Some people tend to blame their problems on other people. The blaming game is a popular game to play. While there are roadblocks and barriers on your path, you should not let them prevent you from reaching your goal. These are obstacles that you have to overcome. They are not merely excuses for your failure. A good leader does not stop when the path is blocked. He unblocks the path and goes on.

You may be an insecure leader when your sense of self-worth is solely driven by results. A person who is results-driven usually wants to see his mission take off. This may yield positive outcomes, but it can also warp a sense of security. You are not secure when your opinions of your own self go up and down with your performance, attendance, comments, reviews, or anything else that other people say about you.

You may be an insecure leader when you are not capable of celebrating other people's success. Do you feel threatened when someone else is favored by your immediate boss? Do you feel genuinely happy about the recognitions and rewards of other people? Do you sincerely want the members of your team to reach their full potential? If you are not secure as a leader, then you are not a good leader. You can say that you have done your job well when you are able to step down from your position with fulfillment in your heart.

You may be an insecure leader when you feel the need to have the final word in everything. If you are not secure as a leader, you tend to be manipulative and controlling. You do not need expert advice because you want to be the expert. Yes, you are the leader of the team. However, this does not mean that you are the best person in the room. Even if you are the CEO, there will still be someone who has a better opinion. You have to be open to these opinions and ideas. Allow other people to speak their minds. When you let other people counsel you, you gain more wisdom.

Chapter 13: Self-Discipline

If you believe that you have the capacity to be a leader but have little experience when it comes to producing actual results, you may not be disciplined enough. Simply put, you can only be a good leader if you possess self-discipline. Your talents will not reach their maximum potential if you do not have self-discipline because it is the one that positions you to the highest level. It is a vital aspect of leadership.

As the leader of your team, you have to form and stick with your priorities. You cannot be successful if you wait for yourself to be in the mood to do things. Likewise, you cannot produce positive results when you wait for things to be convenient before you do them. You need to adjust your attitude. If this is how you work, the members of your team will not respect and follow you. You need to identify your main priorities as well as free yourself from anything that is unnecessary. This way, you will find it easier to reach for your goals.

Also, you have to start and maintain a disciplined lifestyle. In order for you to be successful, you have to realize that having self-discipline is not done overnight. It is not a one-time thing either. You need to be disciplined for the rest of your life once you have started to cultivate it within you. It has to become your lifestyle. You can do this by starting a routine or a system and sticking to it. You have to concentrate on areas that are vital for your long-term success and growth.

You have to challenge the excuses that you often have. In order for you to have self-discipline, you have to eliminate and challenge your tendency to come up with excuses. You have to confront yourself and tell yourself that all your reasons are just petty excuses. If you really want to go higher, then you need to challenge these excuses that hinder you from being the best leader that you can be.

You also have to stay focused on your results. You should not focus too much on how hard your tasks are, but rather on how rewarding your results can be. If you focus on the opposite, you will feel discouraged. You will only have self-pity if you focus on the difficulty of things.

You can improve your self-discipline by identifying your priorities. You can get a piece of paper and write down the areas of your life that you think are the most important. Then, you have to list down the disciplines that you have to form in order for you to keep growing in these areas. You also need to devise a plan that can make these disciplines a regular part of your life.

You also have to know the advantages of self-discipline and write them down. Do not forget to list down the advantages of practicing these disciplines. You should post your list in a place where you can easily see it. This way, you will be reminded of it every time you look at it. Each time you feel tempted to throw in the towel, you should read this list. You should not quit.

Get rid of your excuses. As you have read previously, giving in to your excuses only result in self-pity and negative outcomes. Just like the advantages of self-discipline, you also have to write down the excuses that you usually have that prevent you from reaching a high level of self-discipline. List down these reasons and figure out why you cannot follow through with your plans. Even though they seem legitimate, you still have to challenge yourself and make yourself look for solutions. You need to overcome these excuses.

Leadership and Self-Discipline

It is true that anyone can aspire to be a leader, but only a few can actually be one. Leadership is learnable. So, you can start off as weak and then come out as strong. You just have to have self-discipline and hard work. Do not think that that is just the way you are. If you lack self-discipline, you have to strengthen it. Yes, there are people who are natural-born leaders. However, this does not mean that you cannot be like them. A lot of successful leaders are actually made by self-development and hard work.

You have the power to develop a leadership style and quality that you think are necessary and desirable. This may seem easy for some people and difficult for others. For every person, however, there is an ability to form his personality and character. You just have to be clear about your intent. You also have to be determined towards overcoming setbacks, difficulties, and resistance.

When it comes to developing the style of leadership that you want, you have to determine the discipline that is most helpful in your chosen career. You should refrain from changing everything about you in an instant. You cannot form multiple disciplines simultaneously either. You have to focus on developing one discipline at a time. You have to do this until it becomes part of your personality. Once you are able to do this, you can move on to forming another discipline.

Keep in mind that each act of discipline can reinforce and strengthen all your other disciplines. Likewise, it can improve your self-esteem. Thus, you need to be vigilant. You have to program this new discipline in your mind. You have to start to think of how you should act if you have this habit or discipline in you already. You have to think of yourself in a situation in which you wish to practice the style of leadership that you want.

Conclusion

Thanks again for taking the time to read this book!

You should now have a good understanding of what true leadership means and how to be a good leader.

I wish you all the best in your endeavors!

David Barron

References

1. http://zengerfolkman.com/wp-content/uploads/2013/05/ZFA-9-Behaviors.pdf

2. https://www.officevibe.com/employee-engagement-solution/leadership

3. http://www.ansc.purdue.edu/courses/communicationskills/leaderqualities.pdf

4. http://www.oracle.com/us/media1/steps-effective-leadership-dev-1657106.pdf

5. http://recruitloop.com/blog/5-ways-to-become-a-charismatic-leader/

6. http://bizxcel.com/blog-post/why-commitment-matters-so-much-leaders-and-teams

7. http://ctb.ku.edu/en/table-of-contents/leadership/leadership-functions/build-sustain-commitment/main

8. http://www.briantracy.com/blog/leadership-success/self-discipline-self-confidence-leadership-styles/

9. https://www.gsb.stanford.edu/insights/leadership-responsibility-not-power

10. http://www.forbes.com/sites/jackzenger/2015/07/16/taking-responsibility-is-the-highest-mark-of-great-leaders/#34fc04101d0b

11. https://www.trainingindustry.com/leadership/articles/relationship-driven-leaders-focus-on-people-not-power.aspx

12. http://www.forbes.com/sites/glennllopis/2013/11/04/the-4-most-effective-ways-leaders-solve-problems/#9f11d6e2bda4

13. http://www.businessinsider.com/problem-solving-tactics-of-great-leaders-2013-11

14. https://www.entrepreneur.com/article/163590

15. http://danblackonleadership.info/archives/1273

16. http://growingleaders.com/blog/passion-and-leadership/

17. https://www.shrm.org/resourcesandtools/hr-topics/behavioral-competencies/leadership-

and-

navigation/pages/leadershipcompetencies.asp

x

About the Author

David Barron is a performance coach and management consultant from Vancouver, Canada. Through his work, David aims to guide individuals and executives in reaching their personal and professional goals. His personal mission is to live his life better than he did yesterday, and his goal is to make that mission a reality for every other person that he comes in contact with.

www.ingramcontent.com/pod-product-compliance
Lightning Source LLC
Chambersburg PA
CBHW070044210526
45170CB00012B/580